CLOISTER

BOOKS

Cloister Books are inspired by the monastic custom of walking slowly and reading or meditating in the monastery cloister, a place of silence, centering, and calm. Within these pages you will find a similar space in which to pray and reflect on the presence of God.

MENDING
the
HEART

John Claypool

COWLEY PUBLICATIONS
Cambridge, Massachusetts

Published in the United States of America by Cowley
Publications, a division of the Society of St. John the
Evangelist. No portion of this book may be reproduced,
stored in or introduced into a retrieval system, or transmit-
ted, in any form or by any means—including photocopy-
ing—without the prior written permission of Cowley
Publications, except in the case of brief quotations embod-
ied in critical articles and reviews.

Library of Congress Cataloging-in-Publication Data:
Claypool, John.
Mending the heart / John Claypool.
        p.   cm.
ISBN 1-56101-165-7 (alk. paper)
1. Consolation. 2. Suffering—Religious aspects—
Christianity. 3. Guilt—Religious aspects—Christianity.
4. Grief—Religious aspects—Christianity. I. Title.
BV4905.2.C535   1999
248.8'6—dc21   99-19448
                                                    CIP

Sixth Printing

This book was printed on acid-free recycled paper in Canada.

Cowley Publications
4 Brattle Street   •   Cambridge, Massachusetts 02138
800-225-1534   •   www.cowley.org

To Ann
Beloved wife and best friend
who more than anyone else
has mended my heart

Contents

Acknowledgments

In the truest sense, all human creativity is high-
ly corporate by nature. None of us calls anything into being all by ourselves, and I need to
acknowledge that fact in the following "grace
notes" of gratitude.

My thanks to the Reverend Stephen
Shoemaker for initiating this whole process by
sending me Alice Miller's provocative little book,
Prisoners of Childhood.

I must also express my gratitude to Cynthia
Shattuck of Cowley Publications for accepting
this manuscript and for helping to shape its con-
tents into better literary form, and to Vicki Black,

also of Cowley Publications, for adding many of the scripture portions and appropriate prayers.

On the most basic level, I must affirm with deep appreciation the work of my closest working colleague—Marjorie Swanson—for typing and retyping the several redactions of this manuscript, and the effort of my wife Ann in making numerous suggestions that vastly improved what I had initially written.

Without the generous sharing of these five and countless others, what you are about to read could never have come to be. Debts like these can never be fully repaid, only gratefully acknowledged and lovingly affirmed.

Preface

I believe the best way to begin this little book is simply to tell you how it came into being in the first place. Years ago two things happened to me which, upon reflection, brought me several insights that I have found to be most helpful for the living of my life and worthy of sharing with others. One of my deepest convictions is that every gift we receive would make a good present for someone else. Healing truth is meant to be shared, not hoarded or buried. Thus as certain helpful insights have come to me, I am moved to want to pass them on to others.

The first event that prompted the writing of this book was the death of my ninety-three-year-old mother in 1984. She was the most formative influence in the earliest days of my life. My father was a middle-level insurance executive whose work required him to travel away from home most of the time, so we saw one another infrequently as I was growing up. However, even if he had been at home more often in those earliest years, my mother would still have been the greater force in my life; by virtue of her personality and temperament, she was the strongest and most formidable member of our family. I have smiled often at a cartoon I saw in *The New Yorker* magazine in which a man is standing by the crumpled fender of his car explaining to a police officer what had happened, with the caption: "My wife was driving; I was at the wheel." This is precisely how our family made its way down the highway of life, so the death of the one with whom I had interacted most intensely for over half a century was a profound turning point indeed in my life.

A few weeks after my mother died, a friend of mine in Kentucky wrote a letter of condolence and included with it a book by Alice Miller entitled *Prisoners of Childhood*. It had been of great help to him years before in coping with the death of his own mother, and he commended its wisdom to me at that particular juncture of my life. The author claims that most of us emerge from childhood with two profound forms of woundedness. The first of these grows out of the fact that none of us were born to saints: most parents are far from mature when they bring new life into the world, with aspects of their own lives still confused and incomplete. As a result parents often neglect or mistreat their children in an effort to have their own needs met.

That is why most children come out of the earliest stage of life with a sense of grievance against those who brought them into the world and cared for them in this period of helplessness. Of course the potential for grievance does not end there. Given the imperfect nature of the world into which all of us are born, we go on to encounter throughout our lives other flawed people who abuse or neglect the power that is theirs. Furthermore, we have learned our lesson well: we who are not born to saints are far from saintly ourselves, and so the wound of guilt begins to form in the depths of our consciousness almost as early as the wound of grievance. Truth be told, when we look back over our lives we see many things we have done that we wish to God we had not done, and just as many things left undone that we wish to God we had done. So we struggle not only with our sense of grievance toward those by whom we feel offended, but also with the wound of guilt and remorse over the way we have offended others.

It is Alice Miller's contention that we are doomed to remain the "prisoners of childhood" unless we are willing to do what she calls "the work of mourning" by facing our mutual failings and disappointments honestly and finding a way to redeem them. It is said that we human beings do not learn from experience itself but from our creative reflection on experience. We do not have the power to go back and undo or redo the past, but we do have the ability to "reperceive" the past and decide what meaning we will assign to those events for the present and the future.

The insights of Miller's book affected me profoundly. It dawned on me that I was being called to do "the work of mourning" in the midst of a deep experience of grief. My mother's death brought to an end a certain era in my own human saga and called me to come to terms with all that our half-century together had done to and meant for me. At the same time, I was also faced with figuring out how to live into the present and the future in the radically altered context that grief always brings to the experience of the bereaved. For the one who grieves, "the way it is" is utterly different from "the way it was," and my mother's death brought me face to face with all three of the most far-reaching challenges any of us will encounter. Our particular experiences are unique, to be sure, but it seems to me that the wounds of grievance, guilt, and grief come to all of us. As I realized what was happening to me with the death of my mother, I saw it was similar to the deepest struggles with which I had been helping others during my decades of pastoral ministry, and one episode in particular.

I was very young when I sensed I was being called to devote my life to staying close to God and to human beings, and to make the goal of my life bringing God and human beings closer together. This has been the shape of my calling for over fifty years, and the realities of grievance, guilt, and grief have again and again been the focus of my pastoral concerns. I remember one particularly dramatic episode. Early on a Saturday afternoon, a twenty-nine-year-old member of my church, full of beer and angry at his wife over pulling him away from the baseball game on television, backed his pickup truck out of the driveway and inadvertently ran over his three-year-old son. I arrived at the emergency room just as the doctor came out with an ashen look on his face: the injuries had been so massive that the child had not survived.

This tragedy remains in my mind as one of the most painful I have ever experienced. Both sets of grandparents were there at the hospital, along with the distraught mother and father, and the sense of grievance in the air was palpable. Four grandparents and the child's mother were enraged at the father for what he had done, and the young father himself was paralyzed with sorrow and guilt. He had nothing but love for that little boy; the last thing in the world he would ever have done was cut off that child's life so prematurely. He was filled with self-loathing for what had happened just a few hours before and utterly awash in grief. Someone has said that all grief comes back to this: *we run out of time.* Something ends before we want it to. That is exactly what all of us in the emergency room felt at that moment. An irreparable loss had suddenly engulfed each one of us.

What I experienced with the death of my mother in 1984 reconnected me with this experience as well. Grievance, guilt, and grief are all part of our human journey from womb to tomb, and this realization set me on an intensive search for ways that might realistically help with these particular forms of woundedness. Years ago, I heard D. T. Niles suggest that the essence of the Christian life was "one beggar telling other beggars where bread was to be found." That is a fitting metaphor to describe what this little book is about and explains why I have chosen to entitle it *Mending the Heart.* I offer it in the hope that it will help change our experiences of woundedness into occasions for growth and enrichment.

one

The Wound of Grievance

When Other People Hurt Us

Had it been an adversary who taunted me,
then I could have borne it;
or had it been an enemy who vaunted
himself against me,
then I could have hidden from him.
But it was you, a man after my own heart,
my companion, my own familiar friend.
(Psalm 55:13-14)

Years ago I heard Frederick Buechner tell the story of how his father committed suicide one Saturday morning. The elder Buechner had come from a prominent family. He excelled at college in every way, and everyone expected him to have a brilliant and successful career. However, the Great Depression came along and he was never able to get the kind of job he wanted in order to provide for his family as he desired. Finally, in utter despair, he got up before anyone else one morning and carefully closed the garage door. He turned on the ignition of the car, sat down on the running board of the old Chevrolet, and was asphyxiated before anybody realized what had happened. Years later, when people asked Buechner how his father died, he always replied: "He died of heart trouble." Then he added: "This was in a measure true, you see. He had a heart, and it was troubled." I think this is an apt description for all of us human beings. We all know pain and we all have that kind of heart trouble.

Almost every Sunday we begin our liturgy in *The Book of Common Prayer* with a most ancient and wonderful prayer, the collect for purity:

Almighty God, to you all hearts are open, all
desires known, and from you no secrets are hid:
Cleanse the thoughts of our hearts by the
inspiration of your Holy Spirit, that we may
perfectly love you, and worthily magnify your
holy Name. (BCP 355)

Cleansing the thoughts of our hearts is another
way of talking about mending the heart. The
"thoughts of the heart" are different from the
"thoughts of the mind." According to the Bible,
the heart is the very center of personality where all
our feelings, evaluations, and resolves originate.
The heart is the fountain of our being, where both
the scars of woundedness and the wonder of healing balm are to be found. Ideas, images, concepts,
and energies that can make a profound difference
are there. We all stand in need of this kind of
healing.

No pain in life is sharper or more devastating
than when another person acts destructively
toward us or toward someone we love. The forms
that this pain can assume are endless: people can
use their power to hurt or abuse or deface us, or
they can heartlessly neglect to use their power in
ways that could be decisively helpful. People in

other ages spoke of the "sins of commission" and the "sins of omission," and while we may find such terminology rather quaint, these words nonetheless point to a difficulty that is as old as the human species itself. How are we to react when the destructive behavior of others awakens in us a deep sense of grievance? What recourse do we have?

I believe the answer to these difficult questions is to be found in the incredible mercy and forgiveness of God. The New Testament makes it clear that God's mercy is our ultimate resource in dealing with all forms of imperfection. It is in accepting God's merciful forgiveness, internalizing it, and then extending it to all others that the sort of healing that can "mend the heart" does indeed take place. But exactly how does divine mercy work in relation to the trauma of grievance?

Let me begin by saying that it is important to make a clear distinction between the denial of evil and certain strategies for trying to overcome evil with good. Feelings of outrage and anger are most appropriate in the presence of the genuinely destructive. Forgiveness is not denying the reality of evil; in fact, forgiveness begins by recognizing evil in all of its horror. One of the signs that we have the true image of God within us is that we can react vigorously when the fabric of God's creation is violated. There is nothing authentically Christian or humanly healthy about ignoring the reality of destructiveness or thinking that one should passively endure injustice "like a lamb led to a slaughter" as evidence of a forgiving spirit. We have to face the fact that certain forms of behavior are intrinsically evil and they need to be so identified.

Frederick Buechner once described a seminar he attended one afternoon at Union Seminary in New York City. The subject under discussion was the question of moral absolutes, and many of the participants in the seminar suggested that no such thing existed. They contended that all moral precepts were relative—they were merely conditioned by a given culture or a particular era of history. "Some people prefer vanilla, some people chocolate," it was observed, and there was no external criterion by which one of these could be proved morally superior to the other. Buechner was genuinely confused as he left the seminar with all of these ideas running around in his head.

Later, as he bought a newspaper on his way home, he happened to see on the front page of a New York City tabloid the picture of a three-year-old child who had been savagely beaten to death by her mother's boyfriend. Both of the little child's eyes were swollen shut, her body was black and blue with bruises, and her arms were broken. There were cigarette burns all over her body. As Buechner stood there and looked at that image of battering destructiveness, from somewhere deep within he knew, "This is wrong! This is not a question of you like vanilla, I like chocolate. You like kindness, I like cruelty. This is not the way human power was meant to be used, and something in the very structure of reality cries out against it." For grievance to be addressed redemptively, there has to be a clear-sighted recognition of the real difference between good and evil, right and wrong. To deny the reality of evil is in no way the same as offering forgiveness and mercy.

Furthermore, it has to be clear who is responsible for the destructive behavior. Time and time again tiny victims of abuse or neglect will assume they are the cause. Many children conclude somehow that such behavior is in fact their fault, and internalize this belief as a sense of shame. While guilt is the negative feeling we have about the things that we have done or failed to do and remains focused in the realm of behavior, shame is a much deeper and more primal reality. Shame is the negative feeling we come to have about who we are. It has to do not with our behavior, but with being itself—a sense that we are flawed, defective.

I mentioned earlier that Frederick Buechner's father took his own life in an act of utter despair. About a month after his suicide, Buechner's mother found a penciled note in the back of the novel *Gone With the Wind*, which had been published that same year. The elder Buechner wrote that he loved her with all his heart, but said: "I am no damn good." It is significant that instead of saying, "I have done bad things, or failed to do good things," he came to the conclusion, "I am no damn good." Shame can easily develop in response to grievance. It creates what John Bradshaw calls "a hole in the soul" and this, of course, can tragically warp and disfigure the whole shape of one's personality.

Part of the redemptive handling of grievance, it seems to me, is to help people understand that shame is how we *interpret* our situation and not an accurate description of the situation itself. Psychologist Rudolph Driekus has said that "children are keen observers but poor interpreters"; that is, they take in everything that is happening, but because of their limited amount of experience, they often come to erroneous conclusions. This, I think, is how the whole darkness of shame originates. We need to remember how egocentric we all are at the beginning of our lives. As little children, we have scant awareness of the world outside our own consciousness, which means that we make the mistake of thinking that we are the cause of everything that happens. Thus, we are quick to take the blame in cases of abuse and neglect and allow that negative perception to become a heavy stone dropped into the depths of our being. John Patton, a pastoral counselor in Atlanta, does not think we have begun to reckon with the powerful implications of the reality of shame. He believes that many of us begin to feel shame to some degree as soon as we experience the imperfection of our parents, and it is an issue that we cannot afford to ignore. Most priests and counselors are so anxious to get on with the work of changing behavior, Patton claims, that they are not patient enough or profound enough to work with the deeper feeling of shame, yet this is where much of our "heart trouble" originates.

What can we do? St. Paul once observed, "When I was a child, I spoke like a child, I thought like a child, I reasoned like a child; when I became an adult, I put an end to childish ways" (1 Corinthians 13:11). The great challenge of mending the heart is to realize that we do not have to remain "prisoners of childhood" forever. A whole new way of regarding ourselves is possible. St. Paul describes an insight and an understanding that is open to all of us, if we can only realize that what we thought at the age of four or six or eight is not necessarily accurate. The one thing we know about Jesus' adolescence is that he "increased in wisdom and stature." He let go his earliest perceptions of reality and refused to remain the "prisoner of childhood." He "put an end to childish ways," and this is precisely the high calling of God to all of us in every facet of our lives. For the wound of grievance we have the gift of insight, with all its healing power.

In *To A Dancing God*, author Sam Keen tells of being with his father during the very last days of the old man's life. As they were sitting together in a hospital room one afternoon, Sam realized that his father was trying to sort through his life and come to some evaluation of what he had done with his days and his nights. His reminiscences gave Sam an opportunity to say something to his father that he had felt for a long time. "I don't know how you feel about everything you have done with your life," he said, "but I give you high marks for what you did for us four children. You gave to each of us the greatest single gift that any parent could ever give a child: you took delight in us. You always made me feel that you were glad that I had been born, and that you were glad that I was who I was." I would suggest that this "gift of delight" is the very essence of grace, the affirmation that we do not have to be perfect to be good.

We put an end to childish ways when we begin to realize that the great story at the beginning of the book of Genesis is about our lives as well as about the creation of the world. Seven times in that magnificent passage, as God looks at all that was made, we find the words: "And God saw that it was good." If we can only hear this interpretation that God gives to our lives and begin to see our birth and our creation the way God does, then our sense of being flawed or damaged can give way to the realization that we are loved and accepted and treasured by the One who made us. What Jesus heard when coming up from the waters of baptism is exactly what God wants to communicate to every single soul: "You are my Son, the Beloved; with you I am well pleased."

It seems to me that one of the first steps in healing the wound of grievance is coming to see more realistically the true shape of our own experiences. The first task is to mend our perceptions and see ourselves more clearly. The next task, however, is to learn how to see more clearly those who have hurt us; here again, the guiding principle is forgiveness and mercy. What we accept for ourselves we are also enjoined by the gospel to extend to others: "Forgive us our sins as we forgive those who sin against us," we ask every time we say the Lord's Prayer. Such forgiveness is by no means easy, but it has helped me to participate in God's healing by looking at the people who have harmed or neglected me from several different perspectives in order to see them better.

For example, it helps me to look *behind* someone who has treated me destructively and recognize that he or she is just as much a product of the past as I am. The truth is that those who have wounded us are most often those who have been wounded themselves. The stream of human brokenness goes so far back that no final condemnation of any single individual is possible.

At a time in my life when my mother was still alive, I found I was very angry at her for her domineering tendencies until it suddenly dawned on me that such imperfections had not originated with her at all. It has been said that the trouble with parents is that they had parents, too! For some reason before that moment I had never given any thought to my mother's past, but as I began to think about her mother, her grandmother, and her great-grandmother, I realized that the wounds she inflicted on me had grown, at least in part, from the wounds that had been inflicted on her. With that perception, a log-jam of hostility broke free in me that day: I could perceive my mother differently—with more compassion and mercy—by seeing her against the background of her own history.

A second helpful perspective for me is to look *within* the persons who have caused me problems and remember that they are human beings and not just human "doings." When we have been hurt, we tend to focus totally on the destructive things someone has done and thus identify the whole person with one particular action. It takes a measure of mental discipline, but if we can look within, we will see that a single action is not the whole story of anyone's life.

Years ago, when I was serving a parish in a small county-seat town in middle Tennessee, a teenage member of my parish went on a robbery spree with two of his friends, and the three were caught red-handed the next morning. The juvenile judge asked me to come to a preliminary hearing, and I arrived to find the three store owners who had been robbed there also. The first was a mild, superficial sort of person, and he said to the judge: "Look, boys will be boys. I am sorry this happened, but it is not the end of the world. Just give them a reprimand, let bygones be bygones, and let's forget the whole thing." The second merchant was of a very different temperament. He said to the judge: "These are young criminals in the making. I hope you'll throw the book at them—they need to be taught a lesson!" The third owner, a retired schoolteacher who had lost the most in the robberies, had actually taught these three teenagers years before. I will never forget her response. She looked my parishioner straight in the eye and said: "Billy, I am really hurt by what you did the other night, and I want you to realize how wrong it was to abuse other people's property the way you did. I am really disappointed in you, but I am also convinced there is a finer, stronger Billy inside you. Judge, I wish you would find him guilty, but then give him a suspended sentence and parole him to me. Let me see if I can't do something to get in touch with the better stuff that I know is buried somewhere within him." This is the strategy that the judge finally adopted, and it turned out to be a redemptive one. There was more to that teenage boy than this one episode revealed, so a willingness to look more deeply within turned out to be life-giving indeed.

A third vantage point that I have found helpful is to look *ahead* and ask realistically, "What will
happen if I respond to a grievance this way or that
way?" There are always two aspects to every moral
deliberation. There is the question of motive—
"Why is someone doing this?"—and then there is
the question of consequence—"What is likely to
happen if I take this action instead of that?" Every
time we act, we make a difference. We inject some
of our own power into a situation, and it is important to try to think out what kind of difference we
will make. Our first instinct when we are badly
hurt by another is to want to do the same in
return, but when we are seduced into imitating
what we abhor, we only increase the amount of
damage that was there in the first place. Martin
Luther King, Jr., used to say that the logical end of
"an eye for an eye and a tooth for a tooth is a blind
and toothless generation."

Although it may go against all our instincts, if
we can discipline ourselves to look ahead to the
probable result of our actions and try instead to
return good for evil, such a strategy is likely to be
wiser and more productive. If somehow I can find
the strength to "turn the other cheek" and stay

humane even in the face of inhumanity, at least I will not have added to the sum total of evil. Roland Bainton concluded his great study, *The Christian Attitudes Toward War and Peace*, with a wonderful Quaker aphorism: "If, in order to defeat the beast, one has to become a beast, then bestiality has won." The most creative response to any injury is to do something loving and thus introduce a whole new element to the experience of grievance.

Years ago, I saw an old movie entitled *Stars in My Crown* about the life of a nineteenth-century Methodist circuit rider on the American frontier. An elderly black man who lived in the little community that the circuit rider served was one of its most beloved members, for he had taught a whole generation of children to hunt and fish and enthralled them with his gift of storytelling. It so happened that a valuable deposit of copper was found in that community and it ran straight under the little parcel of land on which the old man lived. When several local business leaders came and offered to buy the black man's property, however, he refused—it was the only home he had ever known and all he wanted to do was to live out his life there in peace. Naturally his refusal threatened the whole mining enterprise, and when a great deal of money is at stake, dispositions have a way of growing surly. When the business leaders could not buy out the old man, they resorted to intimidation, posting a note on the door that if he was not off the property by sundown the next night, then members of the local Ku Klux Klan would come and hang him from the nearest tree.

The local minister got wind of what was happening, and the next night he was there at the house with the old man when the hooded figures arrived. He told them his friend knew full well that they had come to take his life, and had asked him to prepare a will to read to them before they hung him. The old man willed the property to the businessmen who seemed to want it so badly, some of whom were standing right there in the lynching mob. He went on to leave his rifle to another person, his fishing rod to a third, and so on down the line, lovingly relinquishing everything he had to those who had come to take his life. The impact of this act of goodness in response to evil was more than even those greedy hearts could stand. One by one, in shameful silence, they turned away and slipped into the darkness. The minister's grandson, at the time a twelve-year-old boy, had watched the whole drama from afar and when it was over he bounded up on the porch and said to his grandfather wonderingly, "What kind of a will was that?" The old minister answered softly, "The will of God, son, the will of God."

The last vantage point, however, and perhaps the most important of all, is the willingness to look *up* and remember the great forgiveness that God has already given each one of us. Jesus once told a parable of a man who was hopelessly in debt to a king (Matthew 18:23-35). When payment of the loan was called for, the man could not meet his obligation, and was about to be thrown into debtors' prison. He got down on his knees to beg the king for mercy and, in an unexpected turn of events, the king decided to absolve him of the whole debt as if every last cent had been paid off. But soon after that, encountering someone who owed him a piddling sum, the forgiven debtor took him by the throat, demanded that he pay up, and had him put in jail. When word got back to the king that the one who had been forgiven so much refused to forgive in turn, he called him in and read him the riot act.

We are most moved to be forgiving of others when we remember the grace that God has already bestowed on us. The best response that any of us can make to God's mercy is to extend to others the same mercy that has been extended to us. Teresa of Avila once asked God, "How can I ever thank you for all the blessings you have given me?" And the answer came back, "By showing love to those who are as undeserving of it as you are of mine." The best motivation for choosing to be merciful to those who have injured us lies in remembering the mercy God has shown to us and choosing to do the same.

During World War II, a Dutch Christian called Corrie Ten Boom and her family were sent to a concentration camp for offering sanctuary to Jews in Amsterdam. Although her oldest sister died in the camps, somehow Corrie managed to survive. After the war, she went on lecture tours all over Europe and told her audience that their only hope for the future lay in coming to forgive each other for the atrocities of the past. In a church in Bavaria one Sunday night, as the members of the congregation began filing out and speaking to her, she saw coming toward her someone she recognized immediately as the guard in the concentration camp who had been particularly cruel in his treatment of her and her sister. The sight of him, she said later, froze Corrie's heart; she suddenly realized that she was incapable of doing the very thing she had just identified as the greatest need of that moment. All she could do was to pray: "O God, from the same great mercy that You have extended to me, give me now the mercy to forgive this one who stands before me." She said that from somewhere far beyond herself, there came an unexpected sense of strength. It moved her arm, it extended her hand, and she was able to clasp in kindness the hand that had once beaten and mistreated her. She was able to look him in the face and give him the gift of forgiveness, for her perception of him had been changed and, now, she could see him through the eyes of God's mercy.

*O God, whose glory it is always to have mercy:
Be gracious to all who have gone astray from your
ways, and bring them again with penitent hearts
and steadfast faith to embrace and hold fast the
unchangeable truth of your Word, Jesus Christ
your Son; who with you and the Holy Spirit lives
and reigns, one God, for ever and ever. Amen*

(Collect for Lent, BCP 218)

two

The Wound of Guilt

When We Have Hurt Others

> *My iniquities overwhelm me;*
> *like a heavy burden they are too much*
> *for me to bear....*
> *Truly, I am on the verge of falling,*
> *and my pain is always with me.*
>
> *(Psalm 38:4, 17)*

Very few things about the human condition are truly universal, but one of them is this: none of us has lived life perfectly. St. Paul went right to the point when he said that "all have sinned and fall short of the glory of God" (Romans 3:23). An old mentor of mine used to tell me, "By the time any one of us reaches adulthood, it is too late to worry about innocence. That era of our life is over and done with. The only question now is: How do we live with our guilt?" For me these words hold a deep truth, not only as I reflect on my own experience, but also as I have observed the lives of others. We face no greater challenge day in and day out than simply discovering some way to live creatively and redemptively with the imperfection that is inherent in all things human. What can we do with all the bad memories that make up the background of this present moment?

Earlier I talked about the wound of grievance and its remedy in the gift of perception, in heeding St. Paul's admonition to "put an end to childish ways." Now I want to turn to the wound of guilt and its remedies. How can we come to terms with the wound of guilt in mending the heart?

Before we can begin, however, we have to be honest about the many ways that we try to evade or shrug off our sense of guilt. One of the most common strategies we use is denial: refusing to acknowledge our own wrongdoings. Anyone who has ever had extensive dealings with an alcoholic or persons in the grip of some other addiction will quickly recognize this particular form of coping with guilt.

Not long ago, moving through a large airport in the southeast, I bumped into a woman I used to know well but had not seen for a long time. Delighted at this chance meeting, I asked about her husband, who had also been a dear friend of mine. The moment I spoke his name, a terrible expression of pain came across her face and she said, "I guess you had no way of knowing. Peter took his own life about six months ago." I was shocked to hear that this man of such intellect and promise, who seemed destined for great achievements, had ended up committing suicide. The two of us stood in the airport with tears streaming down our faces as she told me the story. What had started as social drinking at business functions had grown into a debilitating obsession.

The more his drinking began to affect his performance, the more he drank to try to evade the anxiety and insecurity that his own addiction created. The ultimate tragedy, his wife said, was that Peter could never bring himself honestly to acknowledge the reality of the situation: "What was utterly obvious to everyone else was a veritable blind spot for him. Whenever any of us broached the subject, Peter would get terribly angry and say:'Look, I don't have a drinking problem. If you think I do, you're the one with the problem, not me!' When he was finally asked to leave his law firm, his shame was so great that he took suicide as the way out."

Of all the ways of coping with imperfection, denial is not only one of the most common, but also perhaps the most ineffective. We have to face the fact that only the truth can bless. There is only one Creator. We live in a world called into being by Someone other than ourselves, and whenever we try to substitute our own fantasies for the way God has put things together, we do not break the laws of reality, the laws of reality break us. Denial of our imperfections is the deadliest of diseases. To try to claim that black is white simply because that is the way we would like it to be is a futile endeavor and will never heal the wound of guilt. Only the truth can bless.

Another approach to the problem of guilt that is almost as common as the strategy of denial is the assigning of blame: we accuse other people or other factors and take no personal responsibility whatsoever. This is perhaps the oldest strategy in the world, going all the way back to the garden of Eden, and we resort to it when we can no longer deny our guilt.

I heard recently about a scuffle on an elementary school playground. The teacher in charge finally was able to restore order and said, "All right. I want to get to the bottom of this. How did all this commotion break out?" With that, one child pointed to another child and accused, "It all started when he hit me back!" The truth of the matter is that no real progress can be made in healing our sense of imperfection as long as we point to reasons outside ourselves and evade our own responsibility.

John's gospel tells the story of Jesus teaching in front of the great temple in Jerusalem one morning when he was interrupted by a group of scribes and Pharisees, who brought a woman forward and said, "Teacher, this woman was caught in the very act of committing adultery. Now in the law Moses commanded us to stone such women. Now what do you say?" (John 8:4-5). What does Jesus do? First of all he stoops over and writes something with his finger in the dust. Then he looks up and replies, "Let anyone among you who is without sin be the first to throw a stone at her" (v. 7).

This story echoes another occasion, where Jesus told his opponents that it was far wiser to deal with the beam in one's own eye than to concentrate on the mote in someone else's. In other words, the place to do something creative about evil is in your own life, not in another's. We cannot wipe away our own imperfections by destroying those of others, or resolve our sense of uneasiness over our past behavior by attempting to lay the blame at other people's feet. Every time we point an accusing finger at someone else, the other fingers of that same hand are pointing back at us.

We also try to relieve our feelings of guilt by punishing ourselves to redress the balance and somehow compensate for the evil we have done. I once heard a hospital chaplain say that either we accept the atonement that God has provided for us through Jesus Christ, or we spend the rest of our lives reenacting it. I have known people of great moral earnestness who have attempted this strategy to right the moral balance.

There is certainly more to be said for this approach than for resorting to denial or blame, yet it too is fatally flawed. In actuality, how much is ever enough? I mentioned earlier the young father who under the influence of alcohol accidentally ran over and killed his three-year-old son. In all honesty, how would he ever have been able to make amends to the child or to the child's mother and grandparents? The agony that we send out into the world when we neglect or misuse our power is enormous indeed, and it is futile for us in our finitude to try to restore the balance of justice and make up with any exactitude for the pain we have caused others. Many are the individuals who have gone to their graves still desperately trying to rectify their sins, the destructive use of their own power.

Perhaps the most ominous solution of all, however, is the effort to redeem guilt by allowing our bad memories such free rein that they take us over completely and define who we are. The distinction between guilt and shame once again comes into play when guilt over our past sins and wrongdoing convinces us that we are incapable of doing anything good. Mark's gospel tells a story of Jesus teaching one day in a house in Capernaum, which became so crowded that four men bringing a paralytic to Jesus for healing had to lower him through the roof in order to reach Jesus. As Mark tells the story, "When Jesus saw their faith, he said to the paralytic, 'Son, your sins are forgiven'" (Mark 2:5). Jesus' words may be taken in many different ways, but he might have been saying that the cause of this man's illness was a sense of guilt that had grown into a paralyzing sense of shame. We are not told what sins he had committed: what he had done or failed to do that caused his sense of shame to immobilize him. But I think it is very important to notice what Jesus actually said: "But so that you may know that the Son of Man has authority to forgive sins"—he said to the paralytic—"I say to you, stand up, take your mat and go to your home" (Mark 2:11). After all the dead ends I have mentioned, forgiveness turns out to be the true remedy for the wound of guilt.

What exactly is the experience of forgiveness? I believe it is more like the event of birth than anything else. We did nothing whatsoever to be born into this world. We did not will our way into existence nor in any sense cause this event to happen. We begin our life in history as pure gift. Birth is a windfall, and so is forgiveness. Forgiveness is best understood as God's willingness to give us a second chance at life on the same terms we were given the first time. Forgiveness is the sheer grace and patience and hopefulness of God, which allows us to try again at life even when we have ignominiously failed.

So the true heart of forgiveness lies in the particular nature of God. In the prayer of humble access that is often said before receiving communion, God is described as the one "whose property is always to have mercy" (BCP 337). What if we believed this with all our heart, fixing our hope on what God is willing to do rather than on what we have done or failed to do? As St. Paul wrote, "Where sin increased, grace abounded all the more" (Romans 5:20). Finally, God's goodness is bigger than our badness, and God's willingness to forgive is greater than our power to sin. When he first saw Jesus, John the Baptist said, "He must increase, but I must decrease" (John 3:30), and I believe this is exactly the genius of the forgiving process. If I honestly come to believe that God's mercy is greater than my sinfulness, then I can own everything that I have done. I do not have to deny it, or try to place the responsibility on someone else, or attempt to earn my own salvation by punishing myself. If I will own my sin and then pass it over into hands far more merciful and creative than I could ever imagine, then God is willing to take even the worst that I have done, teach me the lessons that my sin has to teach me, and make something more beautiful in the future than had ever existed in the past.

Another way of putting it is to say that God is more interested in our future than in our past, more interested in the kind of person we can yet become than in the person we used to be. God takes our sins seriously, but not as the last word. God sees our mistakes for what they are, and at the same time knows that there is more to us than those mistakes. Something creative can still be

done on the other side of all our moral failures. Life is not a spelling bee in which we are lined up against a blackboard and given harder and harder words to spell—and if we miss one word we can never play again. If that were the case, there would be no hope for any of us. No, life is much more like the story of the potter in the book of the prophet Jeremiah. The Lord summons Jeremiah with these words:

> "Come, go down to the potter's house, and there I will let you hear my words." So I went down to the potter's house, and there he was working at his wheel. The vessel he was making of clay was spoiled in the potter's hand, and he reworked it into another vessel, as seemed good to him. (Jeremiah 18:2-4)

Only through a process of patient trial and error does the potter eventually create a vessel of genuine beauty. Similarly, God tells Jeremiah:

> Can I not do with you, O house of Israel, just as this potter has done? says the LORD. Just like the clay in the potter's hand, so are you in my hand, O house of Israel. (Jeremiah 18:5-6)

This is the way forgiveness works. It is God's willingness to give us second chances in life on the same terms we were given for our first chances. Just as we did nothing to earn our way into this world, we do nothing to earn forgiveness. It is windfall, pure and simple, and it cuts squarely across the grain of our egocentricity. You see, when I am truly forgiven, I have everything for which to be thankful but nothing about which to be proud. Forgiveness comes to me because of the goodness of Another. The way of forgiveness is the way of gratitude and astonishment. It lets the past become our teacher rather than our judge. Forgiveness allows us to focus on future solutions instead of past problems by substituting the words *next time* for *if only* as we move through our regrets to the way of hopefulness.

The power to make this shift comes from the belief that God is more interested in the future than the past, more concerned about what we can still become than what we used to be. Remember, God takes our sins seriously, but he does not take them ultimately as the last word. God is not a perfectionist, but a merciful nurturer. He will help us to grow patiently toward the person he wants us to be, and is willing to do this saving work step by step, through trial and error, one mistake forgiven after another. Any acts of repentance we do are not to earn God's mercy, but to show gratitude for God's mercy. They can become a concrete way of showing ourselves that we have learned the lessons of the past and are capable of acting differently.

A minister I know understands this distinction very well. Shortly after an older woman in his parish died, her grown son came to him in terrible anguish. "It is only since my mother died that I have come to realize how defective our relationship was," he confessed. "To be honest, we never got along. She never liked me and I never liked her, and after a while the space between us became very cold. I realize now that I did not do for her in her dying years what I should have done as her only son, and I feel terrible about this neglect. The worst part of it is, there is nothing I can do to make it up to her."

My friend did not try to discount any of the son's feelings, which were authentic, but spoke to him about forgiveness as the second chance God gives to us on the same terms as the first. "There is an older woman in our parish who has no children," he went on to say. "She doesn't know how she is going to negotiate the last days of her life. Let me suggest that you begin to do for this woman what you wish you could do for your own mother but no longer can—not in order to earn God's forgiveness but out of gratitude for receiving it, as a sign that you have really received it. In other words, why don't you begin to build at the very place where once you tore down?" The son proceeded to do just what the minister suggested, so that something real and tangible occurred as part of the act of forgiveness.

I think this is what Jesus meant when he said to the woman who had been caught in the act of adultery, "Neither do I condemn you. Go your way, and from now on do not sin again" (John 8:11). Jesus did not demand that she be perfect from that moment forth. It was, rather, his way of saying, "Do not let this experience be wasted on you. Learn what it has to teach you, so the next time you find yourself in a similar situation, you will be different because of what you have done and what in mercy God has done in response."

Excessive guilt can be the shadow side of pride because it puts too much emphasis on what *we* have done and failed to do. Forgiveness, on the other hand, is a recognition of the relative scale of things. The Holy One is greater than we are and that One is full of mercy. When the focus of our attention shifts away from our own performance, it is precisely in such a shift that the amazing grace of God's willingness to forgive takes root in our lives. When we honestly confess our sins and then hand them over into these hands of mercy, something decisive occurs. Every image of forgiveness we have in Holy Scripture is of an event, a decisive occurrence. The prophet Isaiah promises, "Though your sins are like scarlet, they shall be like snow" (1:18). The Psalmist echoes this: "As far as the east is from the west, so far [the LORD] removes our transgressions from us" (103:12). The prophet Jeremiah says, "When God forgives, He remembers our sins no more" (Jeremiah 31:34). When we enter into the experience of forgiveness, something actually *occurs*. Sin itself sets negative vibrations in motion: our sinful actions make a destructive difference in the lives of all who are touched by them. It is equally true that forgiveness also sets things in motion: every act of forgiveness is as decisive as the event of sin. When we let God have our guilt, he does something redemptive with it.

Furthermore, the process of forgiveness is something that goes on continually throughout all our lives. Author Lewis Smede once wrote that we need to learn to receive forgiveness because we cannot forget. We cannot control our memories. How many times in the middle of the night or at a totally unbidden moment has the memory of something that happened long ago flashed into our minds? This being the case, we have to learn what to do with these memories when they come—as they will, over and over. I take a shower every morning but have no illusions I am done with dirt forever. What I do today will have to be done again tomorrow. By the same token, I eat breakfast every morning knowing that I will have also have to eat lunch and dinner—the lasting power of food is very short.

What I am suggesting is that there are certain repetitive processes that we continue to do to keep our physical lives going, and I believe the same is true in this whole process of forgiveness. Whenever a guilty memory appears in our minds, the thing to do is first to own it and then disown it; that is, claim responsibility for it, seek to learn everything it has to teach us, and then pass it over into God's hands. However, if thirty seconds later the same memory reappears, then we are to repeat the same process. It is important to be patient with this side of life and not to grow discouraged, for the business of guilt never gets finally or completely solved. When God forgives, something happens, and God continues to offer this same saving solution because this mercy is everlasting.

All that I know about the wonder of forgiveness can be summed up in something that happened to a friend of mine many years ago when his five-year-old son started kindergarten. In October of that fall, the teacher said to the class, "Would any of you like to make something for your parents as a Christmas present?" Tim, my friend's little boy, held up his hand: "My dad smokes a pipe! I would love to make him an ashtray." So the teacher got some clay and helped guide his fingers until they roughly shaped it into the likeness of an ashtray. She asked him about his father's favorite color and they painted it blue, then put the ashtray into a little kiln. Tim watched with wonder as the work of his hands grew hard and glistening.

When the time for Christmas vacation arrived, my friend and his wife went to the Christmas pageant that was always held on the last day. Afterwards the little boy went to his homeroom and picked up the carefully wrapped package, but in his haste to run down the hall and put on his coat and wave good-bye to his friends all at once, Tim slipped—and the precious package went up into the air then came down on the floor with a terrible breaking sound. When he realized that all the work of the fall and all his hopes for Christmas morning were dashed, the child began to cry as if his heart would break.

My friend came from a military background and he told me later that it made him very uncomfortable to see a male child of his showing such emotion in public. "Don't cry, son, don't cry," he said as he walked over to the little boy. "It doesn't make any difference." But his wife, who was much wiser, came right behind him and said, "You are completely wrong. Of course it matters!" And with that, she swept up the weeping child in her arms and began to weep with him the tears that are utterly appropriate when a precious thing in life has been broken. Her husband watched with wonder as she reached into her purse and got out her handkerchief to wipe the tears very gently from her own eyes and from the face of her son. Then she said resolutely, "Come on, Timmy, let's pick up the pieces and take them home and see what we can make of what is left."

I would like to suggest that in this family drama we have all the choices that are open to us in the face of our experiences of guilt. We may break down and weep in the fear that life really is a competition, a spelling bee in which we get only a single chance. If we lose this opportunity, we have lost it forever. We may try to deal with our guilt by trivializing it, saying that everything is relative and nothing ultimately makes any difference. Then we will wind up emptying life of all meaning and come to the place where nothing matters. Or we may react as the child's mother did and live into the pain that always comes "by what we have done, and by what we have left undone" (BCP 360). She makes no attempt to avoid the genuine pain of that moment, but she also insists there is still a future in spite of the past. There is still something that can be done. To me this is the essence of the Christian gospel when it comes to guilt and imperfection. Because of God's incredible patience, mercy, and hope, we can stoop over to pick up the pieces, learn what there is to learn from them, and then see what we can make of what is left. *Next time*, not *if only*, is God's gracious answer to our admission of guilt, and nothing is more basic to the mending of the heart.

> *May Almighty God in mercy receive your confession of sorrow and of faith, strengthen you in all goodness, and by the power of the Holy Spirit keep you in eternal life. Amen.*
>
> *Now there is rejoicing in heaven; for you were lost, and are found; you were dead, and are now alive in Christ Jesus our Lord. Abide in peace. The Lord has put away all your sins. Thanks be to God.*
>
> *(Rite of Reconciliation, BCP 451)*

three

The Wound of Grief

When We Are Hurt By Loss

Remember, O Lord, your compassion and love,
*   for they are from everlasting.…*
Turn to me and have pity on me,
*   for I am left alone and in misery.*
The sorrows of my heart have increased;
*   bring me out of my troubles.*

(Psalm 25:5, 15-16)

One of the most dramatic events in all the gospels occurred when Jesus went with his disciples across the sea of Galilee to the wild and sparsely populated region called the country of the Gerasenes. No sooner had they disembarked than they were confronted with a human being whom one gospel describes as "a man out of the tombs with an unclean spirit":

> He lived among the tombs; and no one could restrain him any more, even with a chain; for he had often been restrained with shackles and chains, but the chains he wrenched apart, and the shackles he broke in pieces; and no one had the strength to subdue him. Night and day among the tombs and on the mountains he was always howling and bruising himself with stones. (Mark 5:2-5)

Today we would say that such a man was crazy or insane, not possessed by an "unclean spirit." Certainly the fact that Mark sets the story in a burial ground, "among the tombs," is a revealing clue as to the cause of his derangement. In all likelihood, here is someone who has allowed the experience of grief to literally drive him crazy. The demoniac may have brought someone to that burial ground whom he loved with all his heart, and the intensity of the loss was so great that, in a very real sense, he had never been able to find his way out of the cemetery. The death of one beloved person had meant, in effect, the death of all meaningful life for him. I do not think such a speculation is far-fetched at all, for I have known many people over the years who allowed the experience of grief to be the absolute undoing of their lives. There are few moments in our human saga that are more devastating than to love someone intensely and for that person to be taken away in death. Perhaps all grief comes back to this one reality: *we run out of time.* Something ends before we want it to end.

It is also true that grief poses a powerful spiritual temptation, for the simple reason that it cuts squarely across the desires of our hearts. Every bereavement is a Gethsemane of some kind: like Jesus entering the garden on the last night of his life, we go into our bereavement begging God for one thing and come out with the exact opposite of what we have requested. If having our own way seems to us the essence of happiness, grief is the ultimate affront. I have known many people who have gone on to spend the rest of their lives in rage, bitterness, and despair after losing someone they loved. There is no other experience with more lethal spiritual potential than a grief handled poorly.

What is Mark's ending to the story of the Gerasene demoniac? Jesus commands the unclean spirits to come out of him and enter a herd of swine feeding on the hill, who rush down the steep bank into the sea. When people in the surrounding areas hear of this astonishing story and come to see for themselves, they find the sufferer sitting with Jesus, "clothed and in his right mind." When he begs Jesus to take him away, Jesus refuses: "Go home to your friends, and tell them how much the Lord has done for you, and what mercy he has shown you" (Mark 5:15-20). The story beckons us to look more closely at the gifts that the risen Christ holds out to us, which can turn even the most tragic loss into something truly rich and transformative.

One of the biggest problems that we face in coping with grief is the image of death we construct early in our human pilgrimage. I mentioned earlier Rudolph Driekus's insight that children are keen observers, but poor interpreters. He means by these words that our powers of observation far exceed our capacity to understand what we observe in the earliest years of our lives. We take in everything around us, but because of our limited pool of experience, we often come up with interpretations that have no basis in reality at all.

From these perceptions formed in our childhood, two common misunderstandings of death arise. The first is to think of death in terms of annihilation and total destruction, which is an idea that occurs to many children and certainly did to me when I was a young child. At the age of four, my favorite uncle gave me my very first puppy, a round little butterball of a terrier I named Jiggs. He was the first puppy I was able to call my own, and my mother let him sleep with me in my bedroom; from the first afternoon he was given to me, we were inseparable companions. But one hot summer afternoon, only two months after he had come into my life, I went inside to get a drink of water without knowing that Jiggs was trying to follow me on his short legs. When the heavy screen door slammed shut at just the wrong angle, it caught my little puppy between his head and his shoulders and severed his fragile spinal cord. With a cry of great pain Jiggs fell back into the yard and went into convulsions. I tried my best to bring him comfort, but his small body went limp. Heartbroken, I called his name several times and tried to revive him, but to no avail.

For the first time in my life, I directly encountered the awesome reality called death. After my father came home from work we got a shoebox, put the furry little body into it, and went out into the backyard to bury Jiggs, placing a rough hewn little cross over the mound of dirt. From that evening forward, I never saw Jiggs again. He disappeared from my awareness completely and totally, and because I was a keen observer but a poor interpreter, I concluded from that experience that whatever death touches, it destroys absolutely. While Jiggs was still alive I could encounter him with all my senses, but now that the word "dead" had been pronounced over him, he simply did not exist anymore. Through these experiences of loss we come to believe in the equation of death with annihilation—that whatever dies altogether ceases to be, totally and completely.

Now if this is our image of death, then a pri-
mordial *terror* of death is likely to follow. If death
equals annihilation, then it is no wonder that we
recoil at the very mention of this possibility. It
explains why otherwise sophisticated people draw
back from the reality of dying; why so many
adults shy away from visiting the sick in hospitals,
refuse to attend funeral services, or die without
even preparing a will. The thought of death is so
abhorrent that they cannot bring themselves to
get close to it. It is no wonder that the experience
of coping with bereavement is tremendously com-
plicated if the childhood construct of "death as
annihilation" is the lens through which we view it.
This childhood impression of death's power over
everything it touches may well be one of the
"unclean spirits" Mark's gospel refers to in his
story of the man among the tombs.

The other childhood image that easily devel-
ops early on is that of death as a thief, robbing us
of what we love best. I remember vividly that for
days after the loss of my puppy I felt a grave injustice had been perpetrated against me. After all,
Uncle John had given Jiggs to me and this meant
he was *mine* in some special and proprietary sense;

death had no right to come in and take what law-
fully belonged to me. It is natural for our experiences of love to include a dimension of posses-
siveness as well. In popular love songs throughout
the ages, the most common refrain is, "Because I
love you, you belong to me. You are mine and
mine alone." This sense of ownership with regard
to another explains why we react so often to grief
and loss with outrage and protest. It is as if a theft
has taken place. When we are in the throes of
intense bereavement, a sense of anger is almost
always in the air. Accusations are leveled at members of the family, at medical personnel, and—
more often than not—at God, who has become
the object of outrage. People find themselves saying, "What right did God have to take away the
one person who was truly mine?"

If it is true, as I believe it is, that these two
images of death as annihilation and theft accompany children as they move into adulthood, then
one of the challenges of the Christian gospel is to
redeem and expand our adult understandings of
death. Furthermore, I think this is precisely the
shape of Jesus' redemptive ministry when it comes
to the pain of grief, because there are better ways

of looking at this reality than those that seemed apparent to us as little children. In the work of reperceiving, the risen Christ can heal the pain of our grief just as Jesus healed the Gerasene demoniac.

But how will our healing take place? Death, I believe, is one of the ways God has chosen to move us toward the ultimate fulfillment that awaits each one of us. If you stop to think about it, we do not experience life all at once, but in successive stages. For example, all of us start our journey as two tiny cells in our mother's body. There is a holy mystery to that moment when a living sperm interacts with a fertile egg, and when out of that coming together a new organism is conceived and begins to grow. For the next nine months we are housed in the womb, surrounded by protective and nurturing walls, fed continuously so that we know no hunger, and warmed at a constant internal temperature. In fact, one of the first things that newborns experience is a precipitous drop in temperature. No wonder we feel we have come into a cold, hard world!

That place of beginning is beautifully adapted to the needs of the fetus, but then there comes a dramatic moment of separation. From the vantage point of the newborn, it is a death: we are taken from the place where all has been provided and nothing asked of us, and we move with difficulty into a realm that is genuinely different. From another perspective, however, that same trauma of separation is called a birth. Think of how our bodies and minds and emotions can grow and develop in the world of time and space in ways they never could have had we stayed a part of our mother's body. It is obvious that this pattern of dying to a smaller world that we might be born into a larger world is the shape that God has given to our saga of becoming, and that pattern repeats itself as we make our way through life.

A friend told me the story of visiting a man in the hospital whom he had not seen in years and who was in the last stages of terminal cancer. As Charlie lay dying he said to my friend, "You know, I have wondered all my life what it was going to be like to die, and now that I am up close to it, I have discovered it is simply an old friend in new garb. All my life I have had the experience of having to let go of things that had served their purpose so that I might have access to new experiences. I can still remember how I felt that morning in September when I was six years old and started first grade. I knew very little about what the word 'school' meant because this was back in the era when there were no nursery schools or kindergartens, so this was the beginning of my formal education.

"I remember looking out of the window into the backyard as I dressed," Charlie continued, "and having a terrible sense of nostalgia for the sand pile and the swings that had been the world of my happy and sheltered childhood. I knew that there was a big, ominous building not far away called 'school,' but I had no idea exactly what it was. I went that morning with great fear and trembling, but lo and behold, school turned out to be a place where I grew and developed in ways I could not have if my parents had left me with the sand pile and the swings. In school I encountered people and books and ideas and music—my whole perspective on life was profoundly enlarged. Six years later, I faced the same trauma of having to let go of the elementary school where I had become so comfortable to be thrust into an even more ominous place called junior high, and from there to high school and then to college. From that point on the same pattern repeated itself again and again.

"Through the years I have learned something from all this. Every exit is also an entrance. You never walk out of one thing without walking into something else. So even here I have the profound conviction that what is about to happen to me is going to be part of that same basic pattern. I am going to leave the world of time and space, but I believe there is something beyond the gates of physical death that will be exactly right for the growth of my spirit, just as time and space was better than life in the womb and first grade better than the sandpile."

My friend recalled that at Charlie's funeral, as he made that slow and sorrowful journey behind the casket down the center aisle of the church, a great sense of sadness swept over him. He realized again how much Charlie had meant to him and how their relationship as he had always known it was finally at an end. But as he was experiencing the depth of this loss, he looked up and saw over the back door of the nave the fire department's illuminated sign: four letters spelling out *EXIT*. It

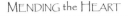
reminded him of Charlie's words, "Every exit is also an entrance."

I find Charlie's story a magnificent statement of Christian hope, for it is rooted in the belief that God's love for each of us is an everlasting love. Jesus said it this way:

> In my Father's house there are many dwelling places. If it were not so, would I have told you that I go to prepare a place for you? And if I go and prepare a place for you, I will come again and will take you to myself, so that where I am, there you may be also. (John 14:2-4)

Death is not annihilation. It does not represent a descent into nothingness. Death is God's way of moving us from one dwelling place into another, a journey one stage further toward God's ultimate intention for us all. If the belief in death-as-transition can take the place of death-as-annihilation, then the whole of our perspective can change. In the words of St. Paul, "Death has been swallowed up in victory" (1 Corinthians 15:54). The One who has created all things loves everything he has created, everlastingly, and we experience that love differently at different stages of development.

God's love for us accompanies us through every stage—from sperm and egg to fetus and infant, then the child, the adolescent, and from there to maturity and old age. There is thus good reason to believe that what happens to us at the end of our lives in history is akin to what happens to us at the beginning; namely, we die to a smaller place that we might move on to a greater. Every Sunday Christians affirm their faith in the words of the ancient Nicene Creed, ending with the affirmation: "We look for the resurrection of the dead, and the life of the world to come." This sense of expectation that there is something beyond the ending of this life is essential to the Christian vision of reality. One of the ways that Jesus helps us to walk *through* the valley of the shadow of death is to cast out that unclean spirit, if you will, of seeing death as annihilation and to replace it with another truth: death as our birth into eternal life.

The other common human belief that Jesus can transform is the idea that death is a thief who takes from us what is ours by right. Once again, the miracle of birth may hold the clue to understanding this aspect of death. I find it helpful here

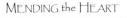

to go back and ask the simple questions: "What did I do to deserve being born? Did I earn my way into this world? Did I cause myself to be? Or is the deeper truth that I was given life as a sheer and total gift? And if this is the secret of my birth, is this not also the secret of everyone else's, too?"

I learned this lesson on the darkest single stretch of road I have ever been asked to travel. In July of 1968, I sat one Wednesday afternoon in the office of the chief hematologist of Children's Hospital in Louisville, Kentucky and listened to words I could hardly comprehend: my eight-and-a-half-year-old daughter was suffering from acute lymphatic leukemia. She had not been well for several weeks, but we had no inkling that her illness was of such life-threatening proportions. When I recovered my wits, I asked the doctor what anyone would want to know in such a moment: "What are her prospects? What chances are there for her survival?" The hematologist was guarded in his response, of course, but in essence he said, "I tell you in all honesty that, at this point in time, the average amount of time from diagnosis to death with this type of leukemia in a child of your daughter's age is eighteen months."

That afternoon marked the beginning of a whole new chapter in my family's life. We did everything in our power to counteract this terrible disease, and we were graced with both medical and spiritual assistance of the highest quality. Yet, in spite of it all, exactly ten days beyond the eighteen-month period, my daughter lost her battle with leukemia. Late one Saturday afternoon, with snow falling softly outside her window, Laura Lue set out on a journey on which I could not accompany her. Her disease was a classic textbook case, and I was devastated by seeing her suffer as she did and then, at the end of it all, to die.

The weeks that followed her funeral were easily the worst string of days I have ever known. People who suffer intense grief will confirm that fatigue is one of the most perennial characteristics of this condition—ironically, although you are completely worn out, you still have trouble sleeping at night. About six weeks after she died, I woke up at two A.M. and was unable to go back to sleep. Rather than toss and turn the rest of the night away, I went down to my study and pulled from my shelves a commentary on the book of Genesis by the German scholar Gerhard von

Rad. For some reason I still cannot explain, I wanted to see what he said about the story in Genesis 22 of Abraham's sacrifice of the life of his son Isaac on Mount Moriah. That story had always been full of darkness and obscurity; to me it represented the last vestiges of paganism, the ancient belief that the first child to open the womb must be offered back to the gods as a form of propitiation. In the Genesis story it is the hand of Yahweh that stops the whole deadly process by providing a ram caught in the thicket to die in Isaac's place. At least that is the best that I had ever been able to make of the story.

But that night the book I was holding gave an entirely different interpretation to the events in this story. It told me that God was trying to discover whether Abraham remembered where Isaac had originally come from. Did Abraham remember that he had never deserved this long-awaited child at all, but received him from a generous God? Did he realize that life is gift, that every birth is windfall, and that all things are here by the graciousness of God? Or had he become possessive of what, in fact, had always belonged to

Another and was given to him out of sheer and bottomless grace?

I remember putting down the book that night as it dawned on me that Laura Lue had come into my life exactly as Isaac had come into Abraham's. I had never deserved her for a single day. She was not a possession to which I was entitled, but a gift by which I had been utterly blessed. And as that sense of her glowed in the darkness, I realized at that moment a choice stood before me. I could spend the rest of my life in anger and resentment because she had lived so short a time and so much of her promise had been cut short, or I could spend the rest of my life in gratitude that she had ever lived at all and that I had the wonder of those ten grace-filled years.

Jesus once promised that the Holy Spirit would help us to remember the things we should never forget, and that is exactly what happened to me that night. As an understanding of my daughter's life as a gift to me began to move deeper and deeper into my consciousness, a long-forgotten memory came to the surface. During World War II, Gladys Meggs, a woman who had lived with us and taken care of our house all through my childhood, left for a better paying job in a defense factory in Nashville. In addition to the sadness we all felt, her departure provoked a small practical crisis as well: we did not have a washing machine, gasoline was severely rationed, and the closest laundry was several miles away. When one of my father's younger business associates was drafted into the army and needed a place to store his furniture, however, we ended up with an old green Bendix washing machine we could use in return for storage space. At the ripe old age of eleven I was put in charge of the family laundry, so for the next four years, every Tuesday and Friday, I practiced the ritual of coming home from school, gathering up the dirty clothes, going down into the basement, and doing the laundry in the Bendix. It was one of those old-fashioned upright models with a plunger in the middle that created all kinds of wonderful configurations of soap bubbles. The wringer was two rubber rollers, operated by hand, and I can remember sticking my fingers between them to see just how far I could bear to go without cutting off circulation. All of this is to say that during those years, I developed a very affectionate bond with the old green Bendix.

In 1945, the war came to an end and my father's business associate returned home. One day when I was at school, a truck pulled up and took all of his belongings from our basement, including the Bendix. No one told me, however, and since it was one of my regular wash days, I gathered up the clothes as usual and went down to the basement. To this day I can recall my sense of utter shock when I saw that gaping, empty space where the washing machine had once stood. I rushed back upstairs in a panic and announced loudly to my mother, "We've been robbed! Someone's stolen our washing machine!"

My mother took that occasion to teach me something very profound. "John," she said, "you must have forgotten how that washing machine got to be in our basement in the first place. It never belonged to us, and the fact that we ever got to use it at all was incredible good fortune. Remember, John, you treat gifts differently from the way you treat possessions. When something belongs to you and it is taken away, you have a right to be angry. But when something is a gift and it is taken from you, you use that occasion to give thanks that it was ever given at all."

I had completely forgotten this experience, but that night, with the commentary on Genesis in my lap and a new sense of life as gift dawning upon me, the memory resurfaced. It came to me that Laura Lue had been a part of my life in exactly the same way. She was a gift, not a possession. My mother's words reverberated in my mind: "When something is a gift and it is taken away, you use that occasion to give thanks that it was ever given at all."

That was the moment I decided to take the road of gratitude out of the valley of the shadow of grief, rather than the road of resentment. To this day I believe that gratitude is the best of all the ways through the trauma of loss rather than a spirit of entitlement. It does not in any way eliminate the intense pain and frustration that always accompany the work of rebuilding one's life in an entirely different context, but it does take away the feelings of anger and the conviction that a terrible injustice has been done, and it opens the way for thanksgiving. Gratitude also deepens our sense of trust, for we begin to believe that the One who gave us the good old days can be trusted to give us good new days as well.

I come back, then, to the story of Jesus healing and transforming the Gerasene demoniac. Here was a man living in a graveyard out of which he could not find his way, but Jesus was able to cast out the unclean spirits that were causing him so much suffering. He replaced them with a new spirit, one that brought the man back to his right mind, with the ability to give thanks for what Jesus had done. Stated another way, this one was enabled to begin to live again creatively in the world that was left.

It is my deepest conviction that if we will allow the risen Christ to transform our childish images of death into his vision of truth, he will also heal us from our grief in ways we do not expect. May the God of all comfort bring these truths home to your heart, and may you find it possible to live again in spite of the losses you have experienced.

Eternal Lord God, you hold all souls in life: Give to your whole Church in paradise and on earth your light and your peace; and grant that we, following the good examples of those who have served you here and are now at rest, may at the

*last enter with them into your unending joy;
through Jesus Christ our Lord, who lives and
reigns with you, in the unity of the Holy Spirit,
one God, now and for ever. Amen.*

(Collect for the Departed, BCP 253)

COWLEY PUBLICATIONS is a ministry of the brothers of the Society of Saint John the Evangelist, a monastic order in the Episcopal Church. Our mission is to provide books and resources for those seeking spiritual and theological formation. COWLEY PUBLICATIONS is committed to developing a new generation of writers and teachers who will encourage people to think and pray in new ways about spirituality, reconciliation, and the future.